PSYCHEDELIC PORTFOLIO

Airliner Liveries of the 1990s

AF572239

CONCORD
PUBLICATIONS COMPANY

Copyright © 1999
by CONCORD PUBLICATIONS CO.
603-609 Castle Peak Road
Kong Nam Industrial Building
10/F, B1, Tsuen Wan
New Territories, Hong Kong
http://www.concord-publications.com

All rights reserved. No part of
this publication may be reproduced,
stored in a retrieval system or
transmitted in any form or by any
means, electronic, mechanical,
photocopying or otherwise, without
the prior written permission of
Concord Publications Co.

We welcome authors who can help
expand our range of books. If you
would like to submit material,
please feel free to contact us.

We are always on the look-out for new,
unpublished photos for this series.
If you have photos or slides or
information you feel may be useful to
future volumes, please send them to us
for possible future publication.
Full photo credits will be given upon
publication.

ISBN 962-361-658-9
printed in Hong Kong

INTRODUCTION

In the early days of airline travel colour schemes were of little consequence, and the aircraft were generally operated in natural metal. Often the only colour would be the airline or operator's titles. It wasn't until the post Second World War period, and the 1950s in particular, that airlines put some thought into their respective liveries. This was the era of the piston engine, and in this period the world's airlines were dominated by U.S. built types, with the many ex-military DC-3s predominant. The Douglas Company was at the time easily the most successful manufacturer with increasingly larger and longer range aircraft being produced, from the DC-4 through to the DC-7. What little competition there was came from Convair with its 240 through to the 440, and the Lockheed Constellation and Super Constellation. In post war Europe the aircraft manufacturers were slow to realise the demand for airline travel, and the Vickers Viking enjoyed limited success.

By now colour was becoming standard on airliners, with the vast majority of airlines adopting the same style, namely a cheatline along the length of the fuselage, usually at window level. Below the cheatline natural metal was the preferred option, whilst white upper fuselage and cabin roof became the industry norm. The individual company logo was usually featured on the tail fin. This pattern was copied throughout the early turboprop era of the Electra, F-27, Viscount and Vanguard. It was also the preferred option of most carriers during the early jet era on types ranging from the Boeing 737, Douglas DC-8 and DC-9, to the Caravelle and VC-10 in Europe.

It was during the 1980s that airlines became more adventurous and employed designers and public relations companies to break with the traditional cheatline uniform. Although most of the new schemes were an improvement, with more use of sweeping curves on the fuselage and more vibrant colours, they were still rather conservative. The mould was broken when Braniff introduced a revolutionary new scheme, which had large airliners like the DC-8 painted all over in vibrant colours, with individual aircraft appearing in different colours, such as all-over orange, red, blue etc. Some were also adorned with additional splashes of colour making them resemble a painter's palette.

The 1990s have seen an explosion in jazzy and zany colour schemes, and it seems some airlines find virtually any excuse now to adorn an aircraft in a special livery. These can be sporting events like the Olympic Games or sporting the colours of a local sports team, the latter usually restricted mainly to North America. Airline anniversaries are a good time to paint an aircraft in a special livery, while partnerships provide an opportunity to paint one carrier's livery on one side of an aircraft, and the other on the opposite side. The 'Star Alliance' has provided the opportunity for each alliance partner to paint up one aircraft to show the livery of every alliance partner along the length of the fuselage. The most outrageous schemes can usually be found on those aircraft chosen as 'flying billboards'. Western Pacific Airlines was probably the first to realise the power of advertising. If a company can spend lots of money on newspaper and television advertising, why not advertise on an airliner which continually visits airports around the country or even abroad. It has been said that Western Pacific received one million U.S. dollars per aircraft per year from companies who contracted to have their colours adorn the side of one of the airline's Boeing 737s. Unfortunately this innovative idea failed to prevent Western Pacific from ceasing operations due to financial problems. The idea has however caught on as low cost Irish operator Ryanair has followed suit, and several of its aircraft appear in the colours of well known companies or products. Even little Aurigny Air Services has painted many of its Trislanders as 'flying billboards'.

In Japan, All Nippon found that when it painted an aircraft with a large whale on the side, people were telephoning to ask which flight the aircraft was scheduled for, simply so they could fly on it! The airline soon realised they were onto a winner, and painted up a second aircraft with a whale to cope with this demand. I still find this strange considering Japan is one of the few nations that still hunts and slaughters these magnificent mammals for so called "scientific purposes". Such was the success of the whale theme, All Nippon has since gone on to paint Disney characters and other such attractions on its aircraft.

For airliner enthusiasts and photographers the 1990s have certainly been a most interesting period. The icing on the cake must have been the British Airways introduction of a new livery which features over thirty different tail schemes from around the world. Those schemes will not appear in this volume as they are now standard British Airways livery. The way things are going, the new millennium is looking an exciting one indeed for aficionados of airliner art.

The following pages feature a number of special airliner paint schemes, the vast majority of which were taken in the last decade. Unless otherwise credited, all photographs were taken by the author. I hope you find as much enjoyment looking at them as I did taking them.

Robbie Shaw, June 1999

PREFACE

I have not included British Airways 'World Images' schemes in this book, as they are now part of the carrier's normal livery. However, to show just how they can brighten up a ramp, I have included this shot of two Boeing 747-400s and a 777-200ER at Gatwick. The schemes are, from left to right ; Colum/Dove from Ireland, Delftblauwe Dageraad/Delftblue Daybreak from the Netherlands, and Vinger/Wings from Denmark.

CHAPTER 1 – AMERICAN ARTISTRY

CHAPTER 3 – ART IN ASIA

CHAPTER 2 – EUROPEAN ENSEMBLE

CHAPTER 4 – AFRICAN AND AUSTRALASIAN DELIGHTS

America West Airlines has painted the majority of its 13 strong Boeing 757 fleet in special colours, a number of which are in honour of sporting teams.

Known as 'Teamwork' this scheme on America West Boeing 757-200 N902AW was the creation of one of the children of a company pilot. It was devised while the company was going through a tough period financially.

The tail feature is given away when it comes to guessing the sport. As a European I have to confess my ignorance of U.S. sports and teams, however I can only assume that the 'Diamondbacks' is a baseball team. Do they play in bottle green? Boeing 757-200 N904AW is adorned in this scheme, and photographed at the company base, Phoenix.

Columbus, Ohio is one of America West's hubs, and Boeing 757-200 N905AW is painted in a somewhat garish scheme to honour the state. It is also named '*City of Columbus*' after the state capital.

This purple and orange scheme on Boeing 757-200 N907AW represents the 'Phoenix Suns' basketball team. It is believed this was the first special scheme adopted by the airline, and it is appropriate a local team has been chosen.

This special scheme on 757-200 N915AW honours the state of Nevada. The aircraft carries the name of two of the state's cities, with '*City of Reno*' on the starboard, and '*City of Las Vegas*' on the port. The aircraft was photographed visiting Los Angeles in December 1995.

Proudly wearing the Arizona colours 757-200 N916AW also bears the name '*City of Phoenix*' after its home base. This aircraft no longer serves with the airline, though the scheme lives on with Boeing 757-200 N901AW.

In 1997 Delta Connection carrier Comair applied special schemes to two of its Canadair regional Jets. Aircraft N954CA wears a paint scheme denoting it is the 100th of the type built. Rather ironically this photograph was taken at Toronto, just a few miles away from the Downsview factory where the aircraft was built.

Although this is the normal colours of the new American Trans Air livery, I feel the colourful tail marks deserve inclusion in this book.

Also photographed at Toronto, and on the same day, is Canadair Regional Jet N979CA heralding the airline's 20th anniversary, complete with balloons painted on the side.

With its home base in Atlanta, Delta Airlines was quick to capitalise and claim its status as the official carrier for the 1996 Olympic Games held in that city. One of the airline's MD-11s, N812DE was painted in a special livery for the event, and named 'The Centennial Spirit'. This aircraft flew the Olympic torch from Athens to Atlanta for the opening ceremony.

Denver based Frontier Airlines operates a fleet of Boeing 737-200s and -300s, but the airline is famous for features of North American wildlife which adorn the tails of its aircraft. Furthermore, each side of the fin is different, adding to the difficulties of those who aspire to collect each different piece of artwork on film. Boeing 737-200 N217US features a Bald Eagle on the starboard side of the fin.

The port side of the fin of N217US features a Mountain Lion.

Taxiing for departure from Phoenix, Frontier Boeing 737-200 N205US has a Fox on the port side of the fin. The starboard side has a Racoon.

A Mallard Duck in flight features on the tail of Frontier Boeing 737-300 EI-CHH seen here about to land at Los Angeles.

Northwest Airlines acquired DC-10-30 N237NW from Varig in December 1997. To mark the alliance between it and KLM, the marking of both carriers were applied late in 1998. On the port side the Northwest livery adorns the fuselage, with the Dutch carrier's logo on the tail. These markings are reversed on the starboard side of the aircraft.

Northwest Airlines has also applied special markings to one of its Boeing 747-400s, N670US. This aircraft, known as the 'World Plane' features paintings all down the fuselage representing some of the many Asian destinations served by the airline. The aircraft is seen here, complete with '50 Years Bridging the Pacific' titles.

This starboard view of N670US gives the opportunity to study more artwork as the aircraft taxies away from its gate at Osaka/Kansai.

A close-up of the artwork on the forward port fuselage depicting a scene from Manila.

Highly successful low-cost carrier Southwest Airlines has the largest Boeing 737 fleet in the world, and an impeccable safety record. The airline has several aircraft painted in special markings, some of which are in deference to destinations served. The airline has three 'Shamu' aircraft painted up with Orca markings advertising Sea World entertainment centres in cities it serves. Illustrated is 'Shamu Two', Boeing 737-500 N507SW advertising Sea World of California.

The fuselage markings of Southwest Boeing 737-300 N352SW represent the flag of Texas, and the aircraft bears the name *'Lone Star'*.

A close-up of the *'Lone Star'* markings, including even the wheel hubs.

With the fuselage adorned in the Arizona flag, it is hardly surprising that Boeing 737-300 N383SW is named *'Arizona One'*. This photograph was taken at Phoenix, Southwest Airlines busiest hub.

The flag theme continues with that of California, complete with Grizzly Bear. Known as *'California One'*, the markings are shown to good effect on Boeing 737-300 N609SW in the Arizona sunshine of Phoenix.

The non-standard silver fuselage colours on Boeing 737-300 N629SW have led to the name *'Silver One'*, in honour of the 25th anniversary.

Freight carrier United Parcel Service (UPS) has painted these large sporting figures on the side of Boeing 747-200B(F) N521UP to celebrate the Olympic Games. This photograph was taken as the aircraft was about to land on runway 13 at Kai Tak, only a matter of weeks before the airport finally closed. The airline has also applied this scheme to a Boeing 757 and 767.

Sadly no more, it was Western Pacific Airlines who set the ball rolling with the logo jet theme, advertising virtually anything for those would pay the airline enough. This shot of Boeing 737-300 N950WP shows the aircraft advertising Stardust gaming resort and casino.

To celebrate the airline's 60th anniversary Air Canada had newly acquired A319 C-FZUH painted in an all-silver scheme complete with Trans Canada titling, the airline's previous identity.

This stunning black scheme was applied by Air Canada to A320-200 C-FDSN to mark the airline's contract to transport the Toronto Raptors basketball team. This agreement however did not last long, but thankfully the aircraft concerned still wears the markings concerned.

The Canadian athlete Donovan Bailey won a gold medal at the 1996 Olympics, and to honour his achievement Air Canada applied his portrait to Boeing 767-200ER C-FBEG.

To mark the Winter Olympics of 1998 at Nagano, Air Canada applied the large sticker of a hockey player to the rear fuselage of A340-300 C-FYLD, seen here leaving Vancouver in very poor weather conditions.

To mark its membership of the 'Star Alliance', Air Canada has chose Airbus A340-300 C-FYLD to wear the colours of the Alliance members. Both SAS and United have Boeing 767s in similar colours.

Known as 'The Signature Plane', and named *'Spirit of Canadian'*, Canadian Airlines has applied the signatures of many of its staff to DC-10-30 C-FCRE.

Seen in a semi-derelict condition at Yellowknife in October 1985 is DC-6 C-CPEG of G.O. Enterprises. The aircraft has the painting of a stagecoach riding through the clouds and the flags of countries visited.

A close-up view of the cloud riding stagecoach and the flags of countries visited. Note too the Kangaroo and Penguin just aft of the cockpit windows.

DHC-6 Twin Otter C-GCGW taxies up the ramp at Vancouver Airport Seaplane Base. The aircraft wears an exhilarating colour scheme and the titles of Sun Express Airlines of the Maldives. The aircraft was on lease to Harbour Air when photographed in June 1998.

Vancouver based Helijet Airways has one of its Sikorsky S-76A helicopters sponsoring the Seattle Mariners baseball team. That aircraft, C-GHJV, is seen during a scheduled service to Boeing Field, Seattle.

Seattle Mariners logo on Helijet Airways S-76A C-GHJV.

To advertise its new electronic ticketing, Aerolineas Argentinas painted the booking telephone number along the side of otherwise all-white Boeing 737-200 LV-LIW, seen here at Buenos Aires Aeroparque in March 1999.

To celebrate the country's participation in the 1998 Soccer World Cup, Aerolineas Argentinas came up with the idea of painting stylised footballers in the country's colours along the side of some of the airline's Boeing 747s. This is shown to good effect on 747-200 LV-YPC at Madrid.

Varig MD-11 PP-VPP was the aircraft selected to convey the Brazilian soccer team to the 1998 World Cup finals in France. The aircraft was gaily decorated in national colours, and adorned with the dates that it had won the cup on four previous occasions. The aircraft was photographed on a visit to London/Heathrow just a few weeks before the finals of the competition began.

Uruguayan carrier Pluna has applied these special and colourful markings to Boeing 737-200 CX-FAT which is seen at Buenos Aires/Aeroparque.

A close up of the markings concerned, an Indian type painting by the artist Carlos Vilaro.

CHAPTER 2 - EUROPEAN ENSEMBLE

Irish low-cost carrier Ryanair was one of the first European carriers to introduce the logo-jet, and the airline has the largest such fleet in Europe. The airline's Boeing 737-200 fleet currently numbers 21, six of which are presently in logo-jet colours. Two of those 'Kilkenny' and 'Eircell' are featured sharing adjacent gates.

Next on the scene was EI-CNT in the orange and white colours which form the logo of two major British tabloid comics (sorry, newspapers), 'The Sun' and the 'News of the World'. The latter is featured on the starboard side, with 'super SUNic' titles on the port side. The aircraft is seen at London/Stansted, the airline's major hub outside Ireland.

The first Ryanair logo-jet was Jaguar Cars, whose British Racing Green colours first adorned Boeing 737-200 EI-CJE in 1996.

The 'Tipperary Crystal' logo-jet EI-CNX appears somewhat bland when compared with other jets in the fleet. It is seen here on take-off from London/Gatwick bound for Dublin.

Wearing the maroon colours of 'Kilkenny – The cream of Irish beer', is Boeing 737-200 EI-CNY. This scheme is very cleverly done, with the nose scheme replicating the head of a frothy beer. Furthermore, at close quarters the bubbles which form the foam can be seen.

The most outlandish of Ryanair's logo-jets is without doubt that which adorns Boeing 737-200 EI-CJD. Introduced in late 1998, EI-CJD features the amazing purple and blue of mobile telephone company Eircell.

A close up of the forward fuselage of EI-CJD with its colourful Eircell logo and statement 'Ready to Go'. There has been conjecture that this was aimed at Go Fly, the British Airways low-cost subsidiary which, at the time, was commencing operations from Stansted and seen as Ryanair's major competitor. If this was so, I'm sure the slogan would read 'Ready <u>for</u> Go'.

This clever feature of a stylised mobile 'phone and clouds' graces the tail of Eircell logo-jet EI-CJD.

The latest, and most highly visible yet of Ryanair's logo-jets is Boeing 737-200 EI-CJC in the bright yellow colours of Hertz Rent-a-Car. It first appeared early in April 1999.

Ryanair has not restricted its special 'one-off' schemes to logo-jets. The first of the special schemes was the thistle and tartan scarf entwined around the nose of Boeing 737-200 EI-CJD (now the Hertz logo-jet). This was for the October 1995 launch of a low-cost London-Glasgow service. In reality however the airports served, Stansted and Prestwick, are at least 30 miles from the respective cities they serve. In fairness however a fast direct rail link, as well as numerous buses serve both airports.

A close-up view of the thistle and tartan scarf on EI-CJD in 1995. Note too the smile painted on the aircraft's nose.

Ryanair first applied Santa Claus to the nose of Boeing 737-200 EI-CJE for Christmas 1994, and has replicated the idea virtually every Christmas since then.

The following year a simplified scheme adorned 737-200 EI-CKS, the only aircraft in the fleet with 'billboard' style logo.

For Christmas 1997 Ryanair adopted a different scheme to celebrate the event. The Santa Claus on the tail and gift wrapping round the fuselage appeared on Boeing 737-200 EI-COA, which had been acquired from Air Portugal in December 1997.

For Valentine's Day in 1997 Ryanair decorated EI-CKS with some appropriate artwork, and named the aircraft 'The Love Plane'. It is seen taxiing onto Gate 6 at Gatwick's South Terminal.

Some of the Valentine Day artwork which decorated Ryanair Boeing 737-200 EI-CKS for about a month in 1997.

In the run-up to Christmas several British charter companies operate flights to Lapland for the benefit of some of the many children who wish to visit Santa Claus. This shot of Air 2000 Airbus A320-200 G-OOAB was taken on Christmas Day 1993, and shows a pair of Reindeer antlers painted above the flight deck windows.

To mark its link with the large Thomas Cook travel chain AirWorld applied those markings to Airbus A321-200 G-BXAW in February 1998. Since then however the airline has been acquired and amalgamated into the fleet of Flying Colours.

For several years now Jersey based Aurigny Air Services has had nose and eyes painted on one of its Britten-Norman BN-2A Trislanders, and named the aircraft 'Joey'. This aircraft has proved popular with local schoolchildren. It is seen at its Jersey base with the appropriate registration G-JOEY.

Aurigny Air Services has recently joined the logo-jet club, realising that flying advertisements can bring substantial income. BN-2A Trislander G-BEVT is seen in Islands' Insurance colours at Southampton in August 1998.

In the colours of Steeple Finance, Aurigny BN-2A Trislander G-BEPH prepares to land on runway 02 at Southampton.

As you might have guessed by now, the Channel Islands are awash with banking and finance institutions. Yet another to display its colours on an Aurigny BN-2A Trislander is SG Hambros, seen on G-BEPI.

British Airways workers at Gatwick who enjoyed running and jogging raised a considerable sum of money for a Rumanian orphanage, and this was presented in time for Christmas 1996. The money was flown out for presentation on Boeing 737-400 G-DOCS, which received these special markings for the event.

For the past few years British Airways has marked Remembrance Day by applying a large Poppy logo to the tail of one of its aircraft – usually one which predominately operates domestic services. In 1996 the markings were applied to Boeing 757 G-BIKC '*Edinburgh Castle*'.

In 1997 the airline took the opportunity to apply the Poppy to one of its aircraft painted in the new livery. This was Gatwick based Boeing 737-200 G-BKYG, an aircraft which has since left the fleet.

In 1998 once again it was a Gatwick based Boeing 737 chosen to bear the 'Pause to Remember' titles and Poppy. This time it was former Dan-Air series -400 G-BVNM.

For many years now the British Post Office has realised that using aircraft rather than trains is a much more effective and faster way to move much of its mail and parcels. Contracts were signed with several operators, and some aircraft were painted 'Post Office Red', sometimes with additional titles like Parcel Force, the division which, not unnaturally, is concerned with the movement of parcels. These titles are seen here on Flightline's Embraer EMB-110 Bandeirante G-FLTY, photographed at Aberdeen, a long way from home.

Aircraft that appear in Post Office colours are devoid of titles identifying their owners. This rather colourful BAe748, G-BEJE belongs to Liverpool based Emerald Airways, but was photographed at Edinburgh.

The absence of the yellow trim detracts from the appearance of BAe748 G-OPFW seen at Bournemouth's Hurn airport. This time 'Owned and operated by Emerald Airways' appears in small letters on the lower forward fuselage.

Sadly no more, British World Airlines was the last British operator of the venerable Viscount. This classic turboprop was a favourite of anyone who flew in one, and will be sadly missed. Resplendent in Parcel Force colours on Edinburgh's cargo ramp is G-OPFI. A number of aircraft which operated for Parcel Force wore personalised registrations, with G-OPFI standing for Go Parcel Force International.

Batman on Caledonian A320 G-CVYG. One rumour had it that Robin would appear on the other side of the fin, but it was not to be.

The Batman on the fin of A320-200 G-CVYG is not part of Caledonian's normal livery. It was applied for a special charter taking enthusiasts to a Batman convention in Dusseldorf, and was on the aircraft for just four days !

Britain's first low-cost airline is easyJet, and its aircraft are easily identifiable by the bright orange and white livery, complete with large telephone number on the side of the fuselage. To mark the start of a service from its London/Luton base to Inverness, the capital of the Scottish highlands, a large green Loch Ness monster adorned the fuselage of Boeing 737-200 G-BECG. This aircraft no longer serves with the airline, whose fleet comprises of an ever-increasing number of Boeing 737-300s.

Norwegian carrier Braathens has, for a number of years, taken to painting special markings on one of its Boeing 737s. These have been to celebrate the country hosting a sporting event, or more regularly, to mark the onset of summer. In 1994 Boeing 737-500 LN-BRJ was the aircraft chosen to mark Norway's hosting of the Winter Olympics, and the aircraft had 'Olympiaflyet' markings complete with Olympic rings and signatures and the forward fuselage.

To mark the coming of summer Braathens has painted special 'Sommerflyet' markings to several aircraft over the years. In 1993 these featured cartoon type drawings by schoolchildren, and these were applied to Boeing 737-500 LN-BRX.

A close up of some of those markings, complete with the names and ages of the children who designed them.

In 1994 it was the turn of 737-500 LN-BRJ, which featured a yellow nose complete with smile, while numerous balloons adorned the fuselage. Later that year this aircraft would appear in 'Olympiaflyet' markings.

A close up view of some of the 1995 'Sommerflyet' schemes.

Since 1994 Boeing 737-500 LN-BRJ has been the chosen mount for the 'Sommerflyet' schemes. In 1995 it was, again, children's ideas which were painted onto the aircraft's fuselage. These are shown to good effect on 'RJ in the evening summer sunshine at London/Gatwick.

In 1997 Braathens chose a variation from its 'Sommerflyet' theme, instead celebrating the 1,000th anniversary of the town of Trondheim. Each side of the aircraft differed considerably, with many sketches depicting life in the town over the years. The starboard side of the aircraft – again LN-BRJ, is illustrated here.

A close up of some of the 'Trondheim 1000' sketches on the forward side of the starboard fuselage.

The port side of LN-BRJ in 'Trondheim 1000' marks differs significantly from those on the starboard side.

To mark Norway's participation in the finals of the 1998 World Cup, Boeing 737-400 LN-BRI had a footballer in national colours painted on the tail.

To mark Copenhagen being chosen as the European City of Culture in 1996 SAS – Scandinavian Airlines marked the event on MD-87 SE-DIP.

Malmo Aviation – recently taken over by Braathens and now known as Braathens Malmo Aviation, has four of its BAe146 fleet painted in logo-jet markings. The somewhat unusual scheme on BAe146-200 SE-DRL advertises Europolitan Airwaves.

The internet and Web Ware are advertised on BAe146-200 SE-DRD seen about to land at Stockholm's downtown Bromma airport.

The latest of Malmo Aviation's logo-jets is BAe146-200 SE-DRA, seen here in the bold lettering and logo of Sydkraft, a Swedish nuclear power company.

As the official carrier to 'Stockholm '98', Finnair applied the event's special logo to the fuselage of DC-9-51 OH-LYP.

In recent years Finnair has applied special Christmas marking to the forward fuselage of several aircraft, and is seen here on Boeing 757-200 OH-LBS at Lanzarote in January 1999.

German charter carrier Aero Lloyd has got in on the logo-jet concept, with A321-200 D-ALAH bearing the titling and logo of Trigema, a T-shirt and sports clothing manufacturer.

Condor's 'Rizzi Bird', Boeing 757-200 D-ABNF is unmistakable. The aircraft is adorned all over in children's cartoons, and can be seen at many airports of the Mediterranean and Canary Islands holiday resorts.

Condor 'Rizzi Bird', Boeing 757-200 D-ABNF about to depart Dusseldorf with another load of sun-seeking tourists.

Like most members of the 'Star Alliance', Lufthansa has painted up an aircraft in the colours of its alliance partners. The aircraft concerned is A340-200 D-AIBA, seen on take-off from Dusseldorf.

One of Lufthansa Cargo's Boeing 747-200F freighters has had additional artwork applied. Aircraft D-ABZF has had a route network complete with time clocks applied to both sides of the fuselage. The aircraft is seen here landing at Sharjah in November 1998.

Several of Germania's newly delivered Boeing 737-700s are operated in the colours of German tour operator TUI. The operator's colourful logo, complete with clouds and Schone Ferien ! (happy holiday) statement is shown to good effect on Boeing 737-700 D-AGEN.

BASE Business Airlines of Eindhoven have Jetstream 31 PH-KJB painted in an all-red scheme advertising 'The Economist' magazine. As the airline has just become the latest British Airways franchise carrier these markings will soon be removed.

For the 1994 World Cup Soccer Championships, Transavia applied soccer balls in the orange colours of the Dutch national team to Boeing 757-200 PH-TKC.

To mark the airline's 75th anniversary in 1998 Sabena applied special markings to newly delivered Avro (BAe) RJ100 OO-DWD seen here at Dusseldorf.

To commemorate the Austrian millennium, the national carrier Austrian Airlines applied the faces of many famous Austrians along the length of the fuselage of Airbus A321-100 OE-LBB. It is no surprise that Adolf Hitler is not amongst them!

Austrian A321-100 OE-LBB has lost its famous faces livery. Instead a special scheme to commemorate the composer Johann Strauss appeared on the aircraft early in 1999. (SPA Photography)

Swiss carrier Crossair operates both scheduled and charter services with a varied fleet of aircraft, including Saab SF340 and 20000 turboprops, Avro RJ85 and RJ100 regional jets and McDonnell-Douglas MD-83s. The latter type is used solely on charter services, including the 'McPlane' HB-IUH, advertising the McDonald's fast food chain. The food served on board even comes from the McDonald's menu.

Crossair Saab 2000 HB-IZK wore this most unusual scheme to mark the airline's sponsorship of the drama 'Phantom of the Opera' in the city of Basle. (SPA Photography)

Crossair's current Saab 2000 logo jet is HB-IYD painted in colours to mark the town of Sion's bid to host the Winter Olympics in the year 2006. (SPA Photography)

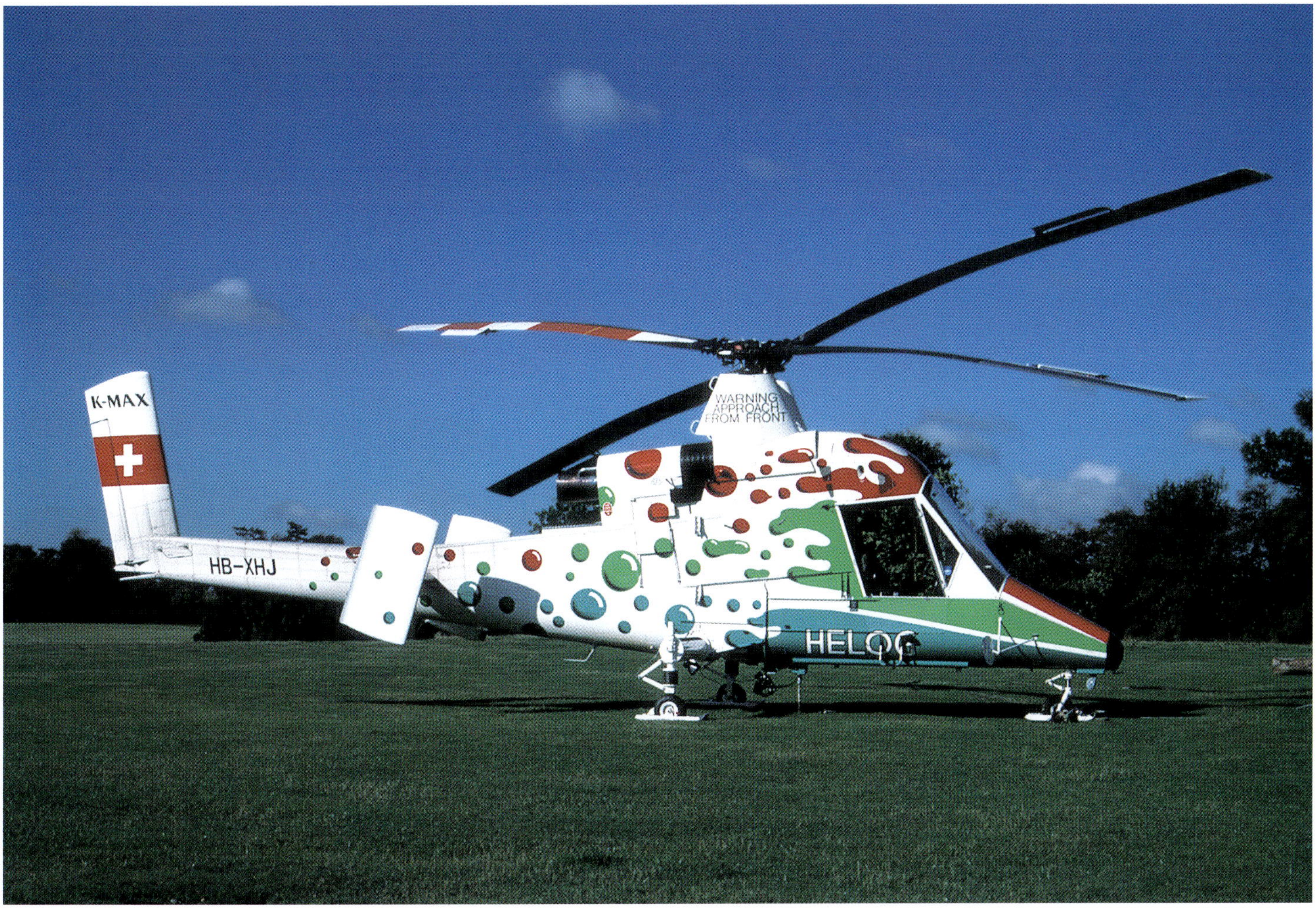

A rather unorthodox yet colourful livery is applied to Kaman K-Max helicopter HB-XHJ of Swiss operator Helog.

This most unusual scheme depicting stars and planets appeared on AOM MD-83 F-GGMB in 1995. The aircraft is illustrated taxiing for departure at Paris/Orly.

The ultimate, and almost certainly the most expensive logo-jet ever, was the Pepsi Concorde. The soft drinks giant acquired the aircraft (F-BTSD) for a ten-day charter in April 1996 to fly invited guests around between some of Europe's capital cities. The aircraft was painted in France in secret and, for the start of the tour was flown into London/Gatwick at night and quickly hidden overnight in a secure hangar. This coincided with the hitherto secret launch of the new Pepsi image in a blue and red can.

The new Pepsi colours on the tail of Concorde F-BTSD.

As France was the host country for the 1998 World Cup Finals national carrier Air France applied a footballer on both sides of the fuselage of 16 aircraft. The colours of each of the 32 finalists were then featured on these aircraft. Airbus A320-200 F-GFKM has the colours of the Norwegian national team on the starboard side.

The Argentine strip appeared on the starboard side of Boeing 747-400 F-GEXA seen here on approach to Kai Tak. The port side of this aircraft featured a footballer in the Japanese colours.

The colourful and unusual markings applied to DC-8-73 F-GDRM of short-lived French charter operator Air D'Evasions. The carrier's aircraft was a frequent operator from London/Gatwick during the summer of 1993.

Cyclists for the Vuelta '96 competition adorned the cabin roof of Aviaco McDonnell-Douglas MD-88 EC-FFJ, seen here at its Madrid base.

Volare Oh Oh ! and the Martini Man appears on the fuselage of Air Europa Boeing 737-300 EC-GEQ. Drinks manufacturers have found aircraft fuselages an ideal platform for advertising purposes. The aircraft is seen on the runway at Lanzarote in the Canary Islands.

To promote the Expo '98 exhibition in the capital Lisbon, TAP – Air Portugal applied this rather outlandish scheme to Boeing 737-300 CS-TIB. The aircraft is seen here at Berlin's Tegel airport.

At the same time sister ship CS-TIB was promoting Expo '98 in Lisbon, fellow TAP Boeing 737-300 CS-TIC was promoting tourism to the Algarve region. This quite magnificent paint scheme is seen to good effect against threatening skies. (SPA Photography)

CHAPTER 3 - ART IN ASIA

To mark the return of Hong Kong to the People's Republic of China, Cathay Pacific applied special markings to Boeing 747-200 VR-HIB which, on re-unification, became B-HIB. The special markings comprised a dark green upper fuselage upon which an outline of some of the Hong Kong skyline was painted. Named *'The Spirit of Hong Kong '97'*, the aircraft is seen here on approach to Kai Tak in November 1997.

With the delivery of new Boeing 737-800s Hainan Airlines has taken the opportunity to revise its livery with a dark blue tail. Some of the flowers which prevail on this tropical island off the south coast of China appear on the side of 737-800 B-2637 seen here at Beijing in February 1999.

Singapore Airlines Jubilee markings to mark a 50th anniversary were applied to Boeing 747-400 9V-SMZ, seen here about to land at Kai Tak.

In 1998 Singapore Airlines began a programme which revamped the cabin interiors of its Boeing 747-400s, particularly those used on the lucrative and high density routes such as London. To publicise the new image the first couple of aircraft received an attractive and colourful new external paint scheme, and these aircraft were dubbed 'Tropical Megatop'. Seen on its first visit to London/Heathrow in this guise is Boeing 747-400 9V-SPL. (SPA Photography)

Singapore Airlines first Boeing 777, a series -200ER (9V-SQA) wears Jubilee markings to mark a 50th anniversary. The aircraft is seen here at Kansai in April 1998.

Air Nippon's Boeing 737-500 fleet feature this playful Dolphin painted on the engine nacelles.

The latest scheme to adorn the fuselages of some All Nippon aircraft is the 'Pocket Monsters', a popular Nintendo game. A single Boeing 747-400(D) and two Boeing 767-300 aircraft feature this scheme, seen here on the former at Osaka / Itami. (Shinya Hata)

All Nippon Airways applied this Whale scheme to Boeing 747-400(D) JA8963. The idea was so popular that many people rang the airline to find out which route the aircraft would be on the next day, and promptly booked a ticket for the flight. This brought in much additional revenue, and the idea was so successful that it also painted the scheme on a Boeing 767, enabling a higher percentage of the population to fly on the Whale jet. I find this rather strange for a country which slaughters thousands of these wonderful creatures every year for so called 'scientific purposes', then sells the meat on the markets afterwards! (Shinya Hata)

Following on from the success of the Whale jet All Nippon applied cartoon characters to the fuselage of domestic Boeing 747-SR81 JA8139. This colourful aircraft is seen on push-back at Osaka's Itami domestic airport in April 1998.

The same characters adorn the port side of JA8139, albeit in different poses.

A close up view of the large characters – complete with snowboards, on the side of JA8139.

'Snoopy' appears prominently on JA8139.

Japan Airlines (JAL) has applied colourful 'Super Resort Express' markings to the side of several aircraft, including Boeing 747-200B JA8141 seen here at Kai Tak. The visit to Kai Tak was rare indeed, as the 'Super Resort Express' aircraft are usually used on the popular Honolulu run. Honeymoon couples are often a high percentage of the passengers on such flights.

A close up view of the attractive bird and flowers on 'Super Resorts Express Okinawa' Boeing 747-300(SR) JA8187. JAL has no less than 13 aircraft in 'Super Resorts' colours.

Both the flowers and birds on Boeing 747-300(SR) JA8187 are pink. This domestic Jumbo variant is used for flights to the southern and tropical island of Okinawa, as displayed by the titling. Most of these flights are operated from Osaka's Itami domestic airport.

The 'Super Resort Express' markings feature birds and flowers, but not always in the same colours. JAL Boeing 747-200B JA8110 has yellow flowers, though the birds remain pink. The aircraft was photographed about to land at Osaka's new Kansai airport.

JAL subsidiary Japan Air Charter (JAZ) operates this DC-10-40 (JA8547) on lease from its parent company as a 'Super Resorts Express' jet, and on this occasion was photographed at Kansai airport. (Shinya Hata)

Japan Asia Airways Boeing 747-100 JA8128 has a feature of women in traditional costumes on its rear fuselage. This airline is also a subsidiary of JAL, and was formed for political reasons, namely to operate flights to Taiwan, which would permit JAL to serve the People's Republic of China without causing offence.

Japan Air System (JAS) used the forthcoming delivery of McDonnell-Douglas MD-90s to change its livery entirely. The result was the introduction of several different, but extremely colourful rainbow type designs. For me, one of the most attractive is that worn by MD-90 JA004D seen taxiing for departure at Itami.

Another variation of the theme is illustrated on multi-coloured MD-90 JA8004 seen at Kansai.

Yet another variation is the predominantly turquoise scheme bisected by the rainbow colours on MD-90 JA8062.

South African Airways introduced the stunning colourful image on Boeing 747-300 ZS-SAJ in 1996. In the national colours, the aircraft symbolises people 'coming together', signifying the multi-coloured society of the nation. The aircraft was used to transport the country's athletes to the 1996 Olympic Games.

A close up view of the rear fuselage of ZS-SAJ.

In New Zealand there are many helicopter sightseeing companies, a number of which have taken the opportunity to paint their machines in outlandish colours. At Rotorua, Tarawera Helicopters have applied the colourful marks to Hughes 369 ZK-HHP. On a helicopter of this type however there is not much area to paint!

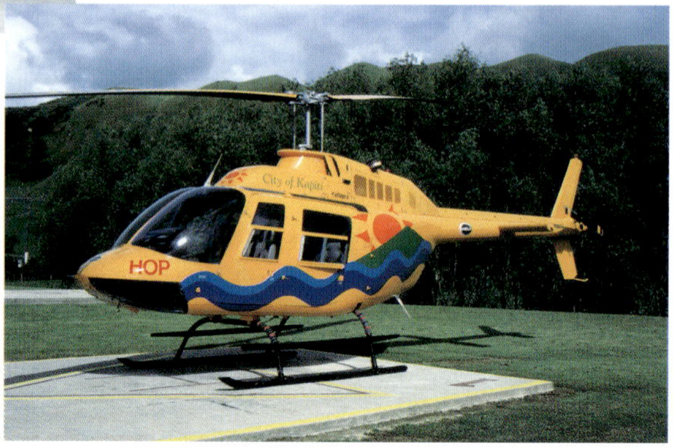

The sun and sea colours features on yellow Bell 206 Jet Ranger ZK-HOP. Named *'City of Kapiti'*, this machine was photographed at Paraparumu at the southern end of the North Island.

Qantas unveiled the qu
adopted by British Airways

Aborigine scheme '*Wunala Dreaming'* on Boeing 747-400 VH-OJB in 1994. The aircraft remains in these colours to this day, and the scheme has been 'World Images' which adorn the tails of the airline's fleet.

Another Aborigine scheme soon followed, this time '*Nalanji Dreaming'* on Boeing 747-300 VH-EBU seen taxiing from its gate at Auckland in December 1995. This scheme too has been adopted by British Airways, and currently adorns the tail of Gatwick based Boeing 747-400G-BNLN.

The Boeing 747 chosen to feature the 2000 Olympics scheme for Ansett is series -300 VH-INJ. This aircraft is one of three leased by the airline from Singapore Airlines, though they are soon to be replaced by leased series -400s, also from Singapore Airlines.

As the official airline for the 2000 Olympic Games to be held in Sydney, Ansett Australia Airlines has introduced special markings to mark the event. These have been applied to the rear fuselage of an A320 and Boeing 747.